C000018763

Say What?

Say What?

Talk like a local without putting your foot in it

Say What?

Talk like a local without putting your foot in it

October 2004
Published by Lonely Planet Publications Pty Ltd ABN 36 005 607 983

Lonely Planet offices

Australia Locked Bag 1, Footscray, Victoria 3011
USA 150 Linden St, Oakland, CA 94607
UK 72-82 Rosebery Avenue, London EC1R 4RW

ISBN 1 74104 454 5

Text and internal illustrations
© Lonely Planet Publications Pty Ltd 2004
Printed through The Bookmaker International Ltd. Printed in China

CONTENTS

If you live in the river you should make friends with the crocodile (see page 69)

INTRODUCTION

Expressions and sayings, idioms and proverbs, they all make up a vital part of language. You probably don't realise how many of these expressions you use every day; they just come so naturally. The word 'idiom' comes from the Greek *idioma*, meaning peculiarity. That's just what fills the pages of this book – peculiarities of languages that we hope will not only raise a few smiles but enlighten as well. There's so much to be learnt about cultures of the world through their languages, and the peculiarities of those languages are surely the most interesting way to learn. While English speakers can feel like a fish out of water, the Spanish feel like an octopus in a garage. While an Australian might have kangaroos loose in the top paddock, a similarly afflicted German doesn't have all the cups in the cupboard.

7

In some cases the foreign equivalents are remarkably similar to the English idiom. In other cases they couldn't be more different. Sometimes idioms originate in one language and are passed into other languages more or less intact. In other cases they are very specifically and culturally relevant to one particular part of the world. For instance, in English the expression 'Pigs might fly' or 'When hell freezes over' is used to refer to something that will never happen. In Argentina the expression, 'On goalkeeper's day' is used instead. Surely this could only have originated in a country where soccer is such a big part of life.

Sometimes we see that two very different languages have surprisingly similar expressions which are in turn very different from the corresponding English proverb. In German and Latvian you discard the spoon when you die, whereas in English you kick the bucket or pop your clogs. In Danish you also leave your clogs behind. In Dutch, where you might expect to find clogs in this expression, the idiom is to 'go around the corner'. Why spoon in German and Latvian but clogs in Danish and English, and corners in Dutch? We can only speculate about how this may have happened. And anyway, that's a different kettle of fish – or is it a different dish of cabbage?

In case your colloquial expertise is still not impressive enough, we've also included some more foreign language expressions. So, let's just say that if mustard begins to climb the nose of an angry French person, it tells us something about their diet. And if that doesn't make any sense, you'll need to read on!

Slip this into your travel bag and enjoy the richness of language in its most peculiar form.

To have kangaroos loose in the top paddock (see page 13)

CHAPTER 1 IDIOMS

This section presents a collection of common English idioms and their foreign language counterparts. So what exactly is an idiom? Well, first of all, you shouldn't take an idiom literally. It's a way of expressing something that pushes the boundaries of how we think and use language. For instance, if someone says to you, 'He's lost his marbles', you could take it in two ways. If you take it literally, you'll understand that some poor boy has lost his little glass balls. If you take it idiomatically, you'll understand that he's gone crazy.

Appearances

His/Her bark is worse than his/her bite

Portuguese: *Cão que ladra não morde*
The dog that barks doesn't bite

Russian: Не так страшен черт, как его малюют
(nye tak stra-shen chyort ka e-vo ma-lyoo-yoot)
The devil isn't as black as he's painted

Avoidance

To beat around the bush

German: *Um den heißen Brei herumreden*
To talk around the hot oats

Czech: *Chodit jako kočka kolem horké kaše*
To walk around hot porridge like a cat

French: *Tourner autour du pot*
To turn around the pot

Calm

As cool as a cucumber

Croatian: *Nije ni trepnuo*
He did not blink

Czech: *S klidem Angličana*
As calm as an Englishman

German: *Die Ruhe selbst sein*
To be calmness itself

Crazy

He/She has kangaroos loose in the top paddock; He's/She's a few sandwiches short of a picnic; He's/She's not the full quid

Finnish: *Hänellä ei ole kaikki kotona*
He doesn't have everything at home

Portuguese: *Cabeça d'alho xoxo*
He has a head of rotten garlic

German: *Er hat nicht alle Tassen im Schrank*
He doesn't have all the cups in the cupboard

Hungarian: *Nincs ki mind a négy kereke*
He hasn't got all four wheels out

Dutch: *Hij/Zij heeft ze niet alle vijf op een rij*
He/She doesn't have all five in a row [The 'five' here refers to the five senses]

Slovenian: *Eno kolesce mu manjka*
He's missing a wheel

To have bats in the belfry

Danish: *At have rotter på loftet*
To have rats in the attic

French: *Avoir une araignée au plafond*
To have a spider on the ceiling

Latvian: *Putniņš bēniņos*
To have birds in the attic

Croatian: *Vrane su mu popile mozak*
Crows have drunk his brain

To lose your marbles

Icelandic: *Að ganga af göflunum*
To walk off the gables; To walk off the edge

Russian: Крыша съехала
(kry-sha sye-kha-la)
His/Her roof has slid off

Filipino: *Masiraan ng ulo*
To have a broken head

Turkish: *Keçileri kaçırma*
To kidnap the goats

Conceit

To blow your own trumpet/horn

Czech: *Vytahovat se jak kšandy*
To stretch yourself like braces

Spanish: *Echarse flores*
To throw flowers to yourself

Dutch: *Hoog van de toren blazen*
To blow high from the tower

He/She has airs above his/her station

Spanish: *No necesita abuela*
He/She doesn't need a grandmother (to pay him/her compliments)

French: *Il ne se mouche pas du pied*
He doesn't wipe his nose with his foot

Danish: *Benene når ikke ned til jorden*
His legs don't reach the ground

Death
To kick the bucket; To buy the farm; To cash in your chips; To pop your clogs

German: *Den Löffel abgeben*
To give away the spoon

Czech: *Natáhnout bačkory*
To stretch the slippers

Swedish: *Att trilla av pinnen*
To fall off the stick

Latvian: *Nolikt karoti*
To put down the spoon

Dutch: *Het hoekje omgaan*
To go around the corner

Danish: *Stille træskoene*
To leave your clogs behind

To push up daisies

German: *Sich die Radieschen von unten angucken*
To look at the radishes from below

French: *Manger les pissenlits par la racine*
To eat dandelions by the roots

Difference
That's a different kettle of fish

Spanish: *Eso es harina de otro costal*
That's flour from a different sack

Hungarian: *Ez más káposzta*
This is a different dish of cabbage

Italian: *Quello è un altro paio di maniche*
That's another pair of sleeves

Difficulties
Between a rock and a hard place

Danish: *En lus mellem to negle*
A louse between two nails

Spanish: *Entre la espada y la pared*
Between the sword and the wall

Hebrew: בן הפטיש לסדן
(bein hapatish la sadan)
Between a hammer and an anvil

Out of the frying pan, into the fire

Thai: หนีเสือปะจระเข้
(nĕe sĕu-a bà jà-rá-kêh)
Escape the tiger, meet the crocodile

Danish: *Fra asken til ilden*
From the ash into the fire

Czech: *Dostat se z bláta do louže*
Out of the mud, into the puddle

Indonesian: *Takut akan lumpur lari ke duri*
Afraid of mud, escape to thorns

This is relevant in a culture where walking barefoot is common. You may step in mud but even when you leave the mud you might tread on thorns, where you'd be no better off.

Up the creek without a paddle

Latvian: *Vakars uz ezera*
An evening on the lake [This originates from the idea that you can't find safe harbour after dark]

Czech: *Ani svěcená voda mu nepomůže*
Not even holy water can help him

Danish: *Langt ude at svømme*
Far out to swim

Double Standards
That's the pot calling the kettle black

French: *C'est l'hôpital qui se fout de la charité*
It's the hospital taking the piss out of charity

German: *Ein Esel schimpft den anderen Langohr*
A donkey gets cross with a rabbit

Dutch: *De pot verwijt de ketel dat hij zwart ziet*
The pot calls the kettle black

Drinking

To be as drunk as a skunk; To be as pissed as a parrot/newt/fart

Dutch: *Lazarus zijn*
To be Lazarus

Lazarus was raised from the dead; when someone is passed out drunk, they may appear dead, but they will rise again.

Swahili: *Kupiga maji*
To hit the water

French: *Etre bourré comme un cochon; Etre rond comme une barrique*
To be as full as a pig; To be rolling drunk as a barrel

Czech: *Být opilý jak čuně*
To be as pissed as a pig

Spanish: *Estar durmiendo con la mona*
To be sleeping with the monkey

To have a mouth like the bottom of a bird cage; To have a hangover

Danish: *At have tømmermænd*
To have carpenters [It's like having carpenters working in your head, ie you have a sore head]

French: *Avoir la gueule de bois*
To have a wooden mouth

Slovenian: *Imeti mačka*
To have a tomcat

German: *Einen Kater haben*
To have a tomcat

Dutch: *Een kater hebben*
To have a tomcat

A liquid lunch

Dutch: *Een glazen boterham*
A glass sandwich

Easy

As easy as pie; As easy as falling off a log

Japanese: 朝めし前
(asa-meshi mae)
Before breakfast [This means that something is so easy, you could finish it before breakfast]

French: *Les doigts dans le nez*
Fingers in the nose [This refers to something that is as easy as sticking your fingers in your nose or that you could do with your fingers stuck in your nose]

Russian: Это как дважды два
(e-ta kak dvazh-dy dva)
It's as easy as two times two

Exaggeration

To make a mountain out of a molehill

German: *Aus einer Mücke einen Elefanten machen*
To make an elephant out of a mosquito

Slovenian: *Narediti iz muhe slona*
To make an elephant from a fly

Arabic: يعمل من الحبة قبة
(ya'malu mina al habbati qubba)
To make a dome out of a molehill

Latin: *Arcem e cloaca facere*
To make a stronghold out of a sewer

Much ado about nothing

Russian: Много шума из ничего
(mno-ga shoo-ma iz ni-che-vo)
A lot of noise for nothing [This is also how the Russians translate the title of the Shakespeare play]

Dutch: *Veel geblaat en weinig wol*
A lot of bleating, but little wool

Romanian: *Mult zgomot pentru nimic*
Much crying and little wool

Fear

To shake like a leaf

Czech: *Chvít se jak osika*
To be moving like an aspen tree

Latvian: *Ka punkis us drats*
Like snot on a wire

Fortune
To live the life of Riley

German: *Leben wie die Maden im Speck*
To live like a maggot in bacon

Slovenian: *Živeti kot ptiček na veji*
To live like a bird in a branch

French: *Péter dans la soie*
To fart in silk

Turkish: *Bir eli yağda bir eli balda*
One hand in butter, one hand in honey

Friendship
They're as thick as thieves

Spanish: *Beben agua en el mismo jarrito*
They drink water from the same little jug

French: *Ils sont comme cul et chemise*
They're like arse and shirt

Danish: *To alen ud af eet stykke*
Two parts out of the one piece

Alen is an old type of measure. In this expression you're getting two of these out of the one piece.

Futility

Pissing into the wind

Mauritian Creole: *Batte caca faire mastic*
Beating faeces into putty

Japanese: のれんに腕押し
(noren ni ude oshi)
Pushing against the entry curtain

If the curtain is hanging in the doorway of a Japanese noodle shop, it means it's open for business. If it's not open, then nothing can be achieved by pushing against the curtain.

Finnish: *Ei siitä tule lasta eikä paskaakaan*
It isn't going to be a child or a shit [This means 'you won't get a child or even shit from all this effort' – obviously referring to straining with the lower body]

To carry coals to Newcastle

German: *Eulen nach Athens tragen*
To take owls to Athens

> *Athena, the patron goddess of Athens, had an owl as a companion. In the 5th century BC the city used silver coins that depicted Athena on one side and an owl on the other. The owl in this expression refers to the silver owls on those coins.*

Thai: เอามะพร้าวห้าวไปขายสวน
(ow má-prów hôw bai kăi sŏo-an)
To take coconuts to the (coconut) grove

Czech: *Nosit dřevo do lesa*
To take wood to the forest

Spanish: *Echar agua al mar*
To throw water into the sea

As useless as tits on a bull

Waali (northern Ghana): *Dau bulamaho*
A wet stick [A wet stick is not going to do the trick when cooking food over an open fire in Ghana]

Czech: *To je mi platné jako mrtvému kabát*
This is as useful to me as a coat is to the dead

Hebrew: עוזר כמו כוסות רוח למת
(ozer kmo kossot ruach lemet)
As useful as applying cupping glasses to a corpse

Cupping glasses (rounded, hollow glass bulbs) are sometimes used in the West and more so in Asia, as a medical treatment. Candles are placed underneath them to suck the air out, then the cupping glasses are placed on a body part (eg the back) to draw all the blood to the surface. It is thought that this cleanses the blood and purifies the system.

Ignorance
To cast pearls before swine

Finnish: *Heittää helmiä sioille*
To throw pearls to the pigs

Spanish: *Echar margaritas a los cerdos*
To feed daisies to the pigs

Japanese: 猫に小判
(neko ni koban)
To put a gold coin before a cat

Hindi: भैंस के आगे बाँसुरी बजाना
(bhains ke age bansuri bajana)
To play a flute in front of a buffalo

Impossibility
Pigs might fly

French: *Quand les poules auront des dents*
When hens have teeth

Spanish: *Cuando las ranas críen pelo*
When frogs grow hair

Russian: Когда рак свистнет
(kag-da rak svist-nyet)
When the crayfish whistles

Turkish: *Balık ağaca/kavağa çıkınca*
When fish climb trees/poplar trees

Filipino: *Pagputi ng uwak*
When the crow turns white

Finnish: *Kun lehmät lentää*
When cows fly

When hell freezes over

Croatian: *Kad na vrbi rodi grozdje*
When grapes ripen on the willow

Dutch: *Als Pasen en Pinksteren op één dag vallen*
When Easter and Pentecost are on the same day

German: *Wenn es im Sommer schneit*
When it snows in summer

Italian: *Nella settimana dei due giovedì*
In the week with two Thursdays

Argentinian Spanish: *El día del arquero*
Goalkeeper's day [This is a very culturally specific idiom
from a soccer-mad country]

Slovenian: *Ob svetem nikoli*
On Saint Never's Day

Portuguese: *No dia de São Nunca*
On Saint Never's Day

Incomprehension

It's all Greek to me

German: *Ich verstehe nur Bahnhof*
It's all railway station to me [There are a lot of comings and goings in a station so it's hard to keep track of things]

Czech: *Je to pro mne španělská vesnice*
It's a Spanish village to me

French: *C'est du chinois*
It's Chinese

Indifference

I don't give a rat's arse; I couldn't give two hoots

Danish: *Det bringer ikke mit pis i kog*
That doesn't bring my piss to the boil

Dutch: *Dat kan me geen moer schelen*
I don't care a nut (female screw) about this

Spanish: *No me importa un pepino*
I don't care a cucumber

Portuguese: *Estou-me nas tintas*
I'm in the inks

Inefficacy
All talk and no action

Waali (northern Ghana): *Nubie yom*
Finger farm

This refers to a lazy farmer who just points towards land he says he will farm but never actually does.

Hebrew: נשיאים ורוח וגשם אין
(nesi'im varuach, vegeshem ayin)
Clouds and wind, and rain nowhere to be seen

Indonesian: *Tong kosong nyaring buninya*
An empty water carrier makes a loud sound

Insults
Get lost!

Dutch: *Loop naar de maan*
Walk to the moon

Portuguese: *Vai à fava*
Go to the fava bean

Finnish: *Sukse kuuseen*
Ski into a spruce

French: *Va voir ailleurs si j'y suis*
Go see if I'm not somewhere else

Colombian Spanish: *Vayase a freir espárragos*
Go fry some asparagus

Spanish: *Anda a la esquina y ver si llueve*
Go to the corner and see if it's raining

Latvian: *Ej bekot*
Go mushrooming

Croatian: *Goni se*
Get lost

Intelligence
He's as sharp as a tack/smart as a whip

[This doesn't mean that whips are smart. It's a play on words – when you are hit with a whip it smarts (hurts)]

Greek: τα έχει τετρακόσια
(ta eh-i te-tra-ko-si-a)
He/She has four hundred brains

Latin American Spanish: *Ser más listo que un coyote*
To be more ready/prepared than a coyote

Spanish: *Ser más listo que el hambre*
To be smarter than hunger, ie to outwit hunger

Mess
It's a dog's breakfast; It looks like a bomb has hit it

French: *C'est le bordel*
It's a brothel [Brothels were obviously not considered the tidiest of places at the time this expression entered the language]

Danish: *Det ligner et bombet lokum*
It looks like a bombed outhouse

Vietnamese: Rối bù như tổ quạ
It's as messy as a crow's nest

Misfits

To be like a fish out of water

Spanish: *Encontrarse como un pulpo en un garaje*
To be like an octopus in a garage

German: *Wie ein Fisch auf dem Trockenen*
Like a fish on dry land

Mistakes

To put your foot in it

Spanish: *Meter la pata*
To put your foot in it

German: *In's Fettnäpfchen treten*
To step into a grease bowl

Turkish: *Yarağına yan basmak*
To step sideways on your penis [This is also used to mean that you have put yourself in a bad situation, just as you can imagine stepping on your penis would be a bad situation]

Like putting Dracula in charge of a blood bank

Danish: *Sæt ikke en ulv til at vogte får*
Don't ask a wolf to guard sheep

Persian: گوشت را به دست گربه سپرد ن
(Goosht ra beh daste gorbeh sepordan)
Giving the meat to the cat to look after

Overkill
To take a sledgehammer to crack a nut

Mandarin: 脱裤子放屁
(tuo kuzi fang pi)
To take your trousers off to fart

Danish: *Át skyde gråspurve med kanoner*
To shoot sparrows with cannons

Thai: ขี่ช้างจับตั๊กแตน
(kèe cháhng jàp đák-gà-đaan)
To ride an elephant to catch a grasshopper

Pedantic
Dotting your i's and crossing your t's

Danish: *Flueknepper*
Flyfucker

Dutch: *Mierenneuker*
Antfucker

Mauritian Creole: *Lipou poule*
Chicken louse

German: *Korinthenkacher*
Sultana shitter

Realisation
The penny has dropped

Mexican Spanish: *Ya me cayó el veinte*
The twenty has fallen on me

> *When a call is made from a public phone, the connection occurs when the coin drops into the machine. In Mexico in the 1940s and 1950s all public phones took a 20-cent coin (veinte = 20).*

Dutch: *Zo zit de vork aan de steel*
That's how the fork sits on the handle

Italian: *Mangiare la foglia*
To eat the leaf

Relevance
What does that have to do with the price of fish?

Italian: *C'entra come i cavoli a merenda*
To be as relevant as cabbages to afternoon tea

Similarity
The fruit never falls far from the tree; Like father like son

Hebrew: התפוח לא נופל רחוק מן העץ
(ha'tapu'akh lo nofel rakhok min ha'etz)
The apple doesn't fall far from the tree

Spanish: *El hijo del gato ratones mata*
The son of a cat kills mice

Turkish: *Babasının oğlu*
He's his father's son

French: *Les chiens ne font pas des chats*
Dogs don't make cats, ie dogs don't give birth to cats

Slovenian: *Jabolko ne pade daleč od drevesa*
The apple doesn't fall too far from the tree

Stupidity
As thick as two short planks

Filipino: *Utak-biya*
Fish-brained

German: *Dumm wie Stroh*
As dumb as straw

Cantonese: 你好似一舊飯咁
(nie hochi yat gau faan gam)
You look like a clump of cooked rice [This means that the person is an idiot, lacks initiative and can only do something under close supervision. It's often used as a reprimand]

Mauritian Creole: *La tête camaron*
Prawn-head

Teasing
To pull someone's leg; To jerk someone's chain

Finnish: *Vetää nenästä*
To pull someone's nose

Russian: Вешать лапшу на уши
(vye-shat' lap-shoo na oo-shi)
To hang noodles on someone's ears

Spanish: *Tomar el pelo*
To pull someone's hair

German: *Jemandem einen Bären aufbinden*
To tie a bear on someone

Mauritian Creole: *Ris so laqué*
To pull someone's tail

Threshold
**The straw that broke the camel's back;
The last straw**

French: *La goutte d'eau qui fait déborder le vase*
The drop of water that makes the vase overflow

Dutch: *De druppel die de emmer doet overlopen*
The drop that makes the bucket flood

Slovenian: *Kaplja čez rob*
The drop over the edge

Danish: *Liden tue vælter stort læs*
A small bump tilts a big load

Finnish: *Viimeinen pisara*
The last drop

Weather

It's raining cats and dogs

Greek: Βρέχει καρεκλοπόδαρα
(vreh-i ka-re-klo-po-dha-ra)
It's raining chair legs

Dutch: *Het regent pijpestelen*
It's raining pipe stems

Danish: *Det regner skomagerdrenge*
It's raining shoemakers' apprentices

Spanish: *Está lloviendo a cántaros*
It's raining jugs and pitchers

French: *Il pleut des cordes*
It's raining ropes

Czech: *Padají trakaře*
It's raining wheelbarrows

Too many cooks spoil the broth
(see page 54)

CHAPTER 2 PROVERBS

This section is dedicated to proverbs — those wonderfully didactic gems that were hurled at us as kids in the belief that we would grow up with a better understanding of the world. Well, maybe they did just that. A proverb is a popular saying which imparts a human truth or a wise message about life in general. Unlike an idiom, a proverb can be taken literally, but the truth it imparts is supposed to be applied in a broad sense. These human truths are the same the world over; they just appear differently in different languages. For instance, the English proverb 'Don't count your chickens before they're hatched' appears in Russian as 'Don't divide the skin of a bear that isn't dead yet' and in French as 'Don't sell the bear's skin before killing it.' If bears were found on the British Isles and not on mainland Europe, then no doubt the Russians and the French would be taking a lot more notice of their chickens and their eggs and worrying a little less about bears' skins.

Appearances
Don't judge a book by its cover

Spanish: *Caras vemos, corazones no sabemos*
Faces we see, hearts we don't know

Hebrew: אל תסתכל בקנקן אלא במה שיש בו
(al tistakel bakankan ella beme sheyesh bo)
Don't look at the jug but at what's inside it

Finnish: *Ei koiraa karvoihin katsominen*
Don't judge the dog by its hair

Appreciation
A bird in the hand is worth two in the bush

Spanish: *Un pájaro en la mano vale cien volando*
A bird in the hand is worth a hundred flying

German: *Lieber einen Spatz in der Hand als eine Taube auf dem Dach haben*
Better a sparrow in the hand than a pigeon on the roof [Even though a pigeon is bigger (and meatier), it's better to have a little sparrow than nothing at all]

Slovenian: *Bolje vrabec v roki kot golob na strehi*
Better a sparrow in the hand than a pigeon on the roof

Dutch: *Beter één vogel in de hand dan tien in de lucht*
Better one bird in the hand than 10 in the sky

Swedish: *Hellre en tia i handen än en tjuga i foten*
Better a tenner in your hand than a twenty in your foot

The Swedish word tjuga *also means 'hayfork'!*

Compromise

You can't have your cake and eat it

Swiss German: *Mi cha nid dr Füüfer und das Weggli ha*
You can't have the fiver and the bread roll

French: *Vouloir le beurre et l'argent du beurre*
To want the butter and the money for the butter

Italian: *Non si può avere la botte piena e la moglie ubriaca*
You can't have a full barrel and a drunken wife

Conformity

When in Rome, do as the Romans do

Thai: เข้าเมืองตาหลิ่วให้หลิ่วตาตาม
(kôw meu-ang đah lèw hâi lèw đah đahm)
On entering the town where they wink, wink the same way

Vietnamese: Nhập gia tùy tục
When you're in somebody's house, follow his/her family's way of life

Spanish: *A donde fueres haz lo que vieras*
Wherever you go, do what you see

Danish: *Man må tude med de ulve man er iblandt*
You must howl with the wolves around you

Polish: *Kiedy wszedłeś między wrony, musisz krakać jak i one*
When you're among the crows, you must caw like them

Drawbacks

You can't make an omelette without breaking eggs

Mandarin: 不入虎穴，焉得虎子?
(bu ru huxue, yan de huzi?)
How can (we) get the baby tiger without going into the tiger's lair? [Also meaning 'nothing ventured, nothing gained']

Hebrew: כשחוטבים עצים ניתזים שבבים
(keshkhotvim etzim nitazim shvavim)
When you cut down trees, woodchips will fly

Excuses

A bad workman blames his tools

Polish: *Złej baletnicy przeszkadza rąbek u spódnicy*
A poor dancer will be disturbed even by the hem of her skirt

French: *A méchant ouvrier, point de bon outil*
To a bad worker, there are no good tools

Family
Blood is thicker than water

Czech: *Bližší košile než kabát*
The shirt is closer than the coat

Italian: *Il sangue non è acqua*
Blood is not water

Futility
It's no use shutting the stable door after the horse has bolted

Japanese: 屁をひって尻つぼめ
(he o itte shiri tsubome)
It's no use scrunching up your buttocks after you've farted

Slovenian: *Po toči zvoniti je prepozno*
It's too late to ring the bells after the hail

It was believed that ringing the church bells would send the hail away.

Danish: *Det er for sent at kaste brønden til når barnet er druknet*

It's too late to fill in the well after the child has drowned

Immutability

A leopard can't change its spots

Maltese: *Min jitwieled tond ma jmutx kwadru*
He who is born round cannot die square

Swedish: *Hur man än vänder sig är alltid ändan bak*
No matter how you twist and turn, your behind is always behind you

Russian: Горбатого могила исправит
(*gor-ba-ta-va ma-gee-la is-pra-vit*)
Only the grave will change the hunchback

French: *Qui naît poule aime à caqueter*
One who is born a chicken likes to cackle

You can't make a silk purse out of a sow's ear

Dutch: *Al draagt een aap een gouden ring, het is en blijft een lelijk ding*
Even if a monkey wears a golden ring, it's still an ugly thing

Maltese: *Hanzir taqtalu denbu hanzir jibqa'*
If you cut the tail off a pig, it's still a pig

Spanish: *Aunque la mona se vista de seda, mona se queda*
A monkey can wear silk, but it's still a monkey

You can't teach an old dog new tricks

Portuguese: *Burro velho não aprende nada; Papagaio velho não aprende a falar*
An old donkey doesn't learn anything; An old parrot doesn't learn to talk

Spanish: *Loro viejo no aprende a hablar*
An old parrot doesn't learn to talk

Polish: *Czego Jaś się nie nauczy, tego Jan nie będzie umiał*
What little Jan doesn't learn, adult Jan will not know

Imperfection
Nobody's perfect

Indonesian: *Tiada gading yang tak retak*
There's no ivory that isn't cracked

Portuguese: *Não há beleza sem senão*
There's no beauty without a thorn

Spanish: *No hay miel sin hiel*
There's no honey without bitterness

Impossibility
You can't get blood out of a stone

Dutch: *Van een kale kikker kan men geen veren plukken*
You can't pluck feathers from a bald frog

Romanian: *A scoate apă din piatră*
You can't get milk from a stone

Insight
It takes one to know one

Danish: *Tyv tror hver mand stjæler*
A thief thinks every man steals

Russian: Рыбак рыбака видит издалека
(ry-bak ry-ba-ka vi-dit iz-da-lye-ka)
A fisherman sees a fisherman from afar

Opportunity

The early bird catches the worm;
You snooze, you lose

Slovenian: *Rana ura, zlata ura*
Early hour, golden hour

Spanish: *Camarón que se duerme, se lo lleva la corriente*
The shrimp that falls asleep gets carried away by the current

German: *Wer rastet, der rostet*
Whoever rests is going to rust

Italian: *Chi dorme non piglia pesci*
Whoever sleeps catches no fish

Make hay while the sun shines; Strike while the iron's hot

Vietnamese: Nước đến chân mới nhảy
Don't jump until the flood rises to your feet

Overkill

Too many cooks spoil the broth

Russian: У семи нянек дитя без глазу
(*oo se-mi nya-nek di-tya byez gla-zoo*)
A child with seven nannies gets no attention

Polish: *Gdzie kucharek sześć, tam nie ma co jeść*
Where there are six cooks, there is nothing to eat

Italian: *Essere in troppi è deleterio*
To be too many is harmful

French: *Autant de têtes, autant d'avis*
So many heads, so many opinions

Persian: آشپز که دو تا شد آش یا شور می شود یا بی نمک
(*ashpaz ke do ta shod ash ya shur mishavad ya binamak*)
When there are two cooks, the broth becomes either salty or tasteless

Patience

Rome wasn't built in a day

Irish: *De réir a chéile a thógtar na caisleáin*
Bit by bit the castles are built

Russian: Москва не сразу строиласъ
(mask-va nye sra-zoo stroi-i-las)
Moscow wasn't built all in one go

Polish: *Nie od razu Kraków zbudowano*
Krakow wasn't built in a day

Presumption
To count your chickens before they're hatched

Russian: Делить шкуру неубитого медведя
(dye-lit' shkoo-roo nye-oo-bi-ta-va myed-vye-dya)
To divide the skin of a bear that isn't dead yet

Slovenian: *Ne hvali dneva pred večerom*
Don't praise the day before the evening

French: *Vendre la peau de l'ours avant de l'avoir tué*
To sell the bear's skin before killing it

Don't pay the ferryman until he gets you to the other side

Swedish: *Ropa inte hej förrän du är över bäcken*
Don't yell 'hello' until you're over the stream

Hindi: घर में सूत न कपास, जुलाहे से लट्टम लट्टा
(ghar me sut na kapas, julahe se lattham lattha)
Fighting with the weaver when there is neither thread nor cotton wool in the house

Responsibility

You make your bed, you lie in it; You reap what you sow

Danish: *Man høster som man sår*
You harvest as you sow

Dutch: *Wie zijn gat brandt, moet op de blaren zitten*
Whoever burns his/her arse will have to sit on the blisters

Hebrew: אתה בישלת את הדייסה אתה תאכל אותה
(ata bishalta et hadaysa, ata tochal ota)
You cooked this porridge, you eat it

Slovenian: *Kakor si boš postlal tako boš spal*
You make your bed, you lie in it

Teamwork

In numbers there is strength; Safety in numbers

Maori: *Kaua e rangiruatia te hä o te hoe; e kore tö tätou waka e ü ki uta*
Don't lift the paddle out of unison or our canoe will never reach the shore

Amharic: ድር ቢያበር አንበሳ ያስር
(der bi-ya-ber an-bes-sa yas-ser)
Spider webs joined together can catch a lion

Russian: Вкруте и вяз переломишь
(fkroo-tye i vyaz pe-re-lom-ish)
United, it's even possible to break an elm tree

*Even there, the fence is not made
of sausages (see page 71)*

CHAPTER 3 OTHER FOREIGN LANGUAGE EXPRESSIONS

As we all know there's nothing that will guarantee you stick out like a sore thumb more than a complete ignorance of the local lingo. 'Hello', 'please', 'thank you' and 'goodbye' can help you on your way, but frankly they're not going to impress anyone. Now that you have some idioms and proverbs under your belt you're well on your way to verbal prowess, but this last section will ensure your linguistic success. Pepper your conversation with a few of the expressions in this chapter and you're sure to surprise your new friends.

Afrikaans

Met die deur in die huis val

To fall into the house with the door

To do or say something too abruptly

Amharic

የደላው ሙቅ ያኝካል

(ye-de-low muk yan-yeu-kal)

A person with too much will start chewing porridge

If you have too much you'll end up doing something unworthy or pointless

Arabic

شعرة من الخنزير مكسب

(sha'ariah min al-khanzeer mac'sab)

A hair picked out of a pig is a gain

Something is better than nothing

Cantonese

三 心 兩 意

(saam sum leung yee)

Three hearts, two ideas

Said about someone who lets his/her emotions get in the way of making rational decisions

Cheyenne

Étaoméhótsenôhtóvenestse napâhpóneehéhame

My tapeworm can almost talk by itself

I am very hungry

Creole

Dèyè mòn, gen mòn

(Haitian Creole)

Behind the mountains, more mountains

A big and daunting task

Pa rente dan caless cassé

(Mauritian Creole)

Don't get into a broken carriage

Don't get involved in other people's problems

Czech

Čumět jak čerstvě vyoraná myš

To look like a freshly dug-out mouse

To look bewildered or confused

Danish

Blind høne kan også finde korn

Blind chicken can also find grain

Qualified people are not always the most successful

Stikke fingeren i jorden

Stick your finger in the ground

Test the waters

Dutch

Daar komt de aap uit de mouw
Here comes the monkey out of the sleeve
An important piece of information is about to be revealed

De klok horen luiden maar de klepel niet weten hangen
To hear the bell ring without knowing where to find the clapper
To have only vague or insufficient knowledge of something

Een ballonnetje laten opgaan
To let a little balloon go
To put an idea in someone's head and get them thinking about it

Wij zullen dat varkentje wel wassen
We'll wash that little pig
We'll sort that out or deal with it – said about someone or something that seems particularly difficult to deal with

Met de deur in huis vallen
To fall into the house with the door
To do or say something abruptly

Filipino
Halang ang bituka
He has a horizontal intestine
He has no moral conscience

Namamangka sa dalawang ilog
A boat rowing between two rivers
An unfaithful person [You won't get very far by rowing between two rivers; you should instead pick a river and row on that one]

Finnish
Olla ketunhäntä kainalossa
To have a fox's tail under your armpit
To have ulterior motives

Olla äimän käkenä
To be like the cuckoo of äimä
To be dumbfounded

French

La moutarde me monte au nez
Mustard is climbing up my nose
I am beginning to lose my temper

Péter plus haut que son cul
To fart higher than your arse
To think very highly of yourself

Tu as l'air d'une poule qui aurait trouvé un couteau
You look like a hen who's found a knife
You look slightly bewildered or confused – what would a hen do with a knife?

German

Hinter schwedischen Gardinen sitzen

To be behind Swedish curtains

To be behind bars; To go to jail

Gardinen *(curtains) is a slang term for 'bars'. At one time, the high-grade steel from which prison bars were forged came from Swedish ore.*

Er gibt seinen Senf dazu

He brings his mustard along

He always has something to say, even if no-one else is interested

Puderzucker in den Arsch geblasen kriegen

To get icing sugar blown up your arse

To have things comes easily to you or go well for you

Sich die Beine in den Bauch stehen

To stand until your legs are in your stomach

To wait a very, very long time

So wis i Wald tönt chunnts zrügg

(Swiss German)

Speak into the forest and the forest will speak back to you

What goes around comes around

Greek

άρμεγε λαγούς και κούρευε χελώνες

(ar-me-ghe lagh-ous ke kou-re-ve he-lo-nes)

Milk the hares and give the turtles a haircut

To do something that is a complete waste of time

έχει καβούρια στις τσέπες

(eh-i ka-vou-ri-a stis tse-pes)

He/She has crabs in the pocket

He/She is a mean or stingy person – the crabs have eaten all his/her money

Σαν τα χιόνια

(san ta hi-on-i-a)

He/She appeared like the snow

When someone shows up unexpectedly after a long period of absence

This expression would have originated in a place where it doesn't snow or hardly snows at all, such as Greece.

Hebrew

פה קבור הכלב

(kan kavur hacalev)

So this is where the dog is buried

When the real reason for something reveals itself

This expression comes from the title of a popular song in Hebrew. It's similar to the English idiom 'getting to the heart of the matter'.

Hindi

बंदर क्या जाने अदरक का स्वाद

(bandar kya jane adrak ka swaad)

You can't expect a monkey to know the taste of ginger

You can't expect someone to understand something that is foreign to them [This is also often translated as 'Don't cast pearls before swine']

पानी में रहकर मगर से बैर करना

(pani me rahkar magar se bair karna)

If you live in the river you should make friends with the crocodile

Keep your friends close and your enemies even closer [This is also sometimes translated as 'It's hard to live in Rome and fight with the Pope']

किसी के घर में आग लगाकर अपना हाथ
सेंकना

(kisi ke ghar me aag lagakar apna hath senkna)

To warm your hands on somebody's burning house

What is play to one is death to another, ie one person's idea of fun isn't necessarily another person's idea of fun

Hungarian

Most jön a feketeleves

Now comes the black soup

Now for the bad news

When the Ottoman forces took Buda (the Hungarian capital) in 1541, their victory was announced to the unsuspecting Hungarian leaders after a dinner they had been invited to by the Ottomans. After the meal the Hungarians were asked to have their coffee outside, where they saw the Turkish flag flying high from Buda castle. The black soup refers to the coffee that was served at this horrible moment of realisation.

Ott sincs kolbászból fonva a kerítés

Even there the fence is not made of sausages

The grass is not greener there

Icelandic

Að koma einhverjum fyrir kattarnef

To bring someone in front of a cat's nose

To kill someone or be responsible for their death

The origins of this expression are unclear but it could well be a reference to the Christmas Cat that belonged to the witch Grýla in Icelandic folklore. The story goes that this cat would eat those who didn't receive a Christmas present. That's why in Iceland you would give a little something to everyone in the household at Christmas with the words 'Just so you won't end up in the Christmas Cat.'

Indonesian

Di bawah empat mata

Beneath four eyes

Something done privately, behind closed doors

Italian

Fare un quarantotto

To make a 48

To make a great mess of something; To raise hell

This is a reference to the year 1848 which was a time of revolt in much of Europe.

Non cavare un ragno dal buco

Not to be able to take a spider out of a hole

To draw a blank

Non c'è trippa per gatti
There's no tripe for the cats
To tighten one's belt; To be the end of the matter

When Ernesto Nathan became ruler of Rome in 1907 he decided to sort out the budget. As part of his cuts to expenditure he cancelled a standing order for tripe, and the usually lucky cats of the Colosseum had to go without.

Japanese
猿も木から落ちる
(saru mo ki kara ochiru)
Even monkeys fall out of trees
Everyone makes mistakes

Lao

ເລືອກຊ້າງ ໃຫ້ເບິ່ງຫາງ ເລືອກງາງ ໃຫ້ເບິ່ງແມ່

(lêu-ak sâhng hâi beung hăhng lêu-ak nâhng hâi beung maa)

When choosing an elephant check the tail

When choosing a wife look at her mother

Latin

Faber est suae quisque fortunae

Everyone is the blacksmith of his/her own destiny

A blacksmith shapes and moulds metal into something he/she wants it to be, just as we make choices that shape our lives

Hic Rodus hic salta!

Here is Rhodes, jump here!

This expression is used when someone is blowing their own trumpet and needs to be taken down a peg or two (to use a couple of other idioms)

This comes from an Aesop fable in which a vain man, on his return home from Rhodes, boasted to his friends that while away he had done some amazingly long jumps. When they asked him to prove it by doing an impressive jump for them, his failure revealed him to be a fraud.

Latvian

Ar gariem zobiem
With long teeth

When you do something that is unpleasant to you, it's said you do it 'with long teeth'

This comes from the idea that when you taste something you don't like, you just touch it with your teeth.

Malay

Bermain kayu tiga

Playing with three sticks

Two-timing your partner

Maltese

Iz-zalza ghola mill-huta

The sauce is more expensive than the fish

Spending more time or money on trimmings than on the object itself

Mandarin

指鹿为马

(zhi lu wei ma)

Point at a deer and call it a horse

To submit to a powerful person's will rather than do what's right

A powerful and cruel emperor wanted to test the loyalty of his courtiers by bringing a deer into the court and calling it a horse. He asked each person what they thought it was – those who said it was a deer were killed.

守株待兔

(shou zhu dai tu)

Like a hunter waiting for a rabbit to kill itself by running into a tree

Trusting in dumb luck, hoping that the almost impossible will happen and solve any problems

This goes back to the true story of a rabbit that actually did have a freak accident and killed itself by running into a tree – from then onwards the hunter was convinced this would happen again.

坐井观天

(zuo jing guan tian)

It's like looking at the sky from the bottom of a well

Not seeing the whole picture

此地无银三百两，隔壁阿二不曾偷

(cidi wu yin sanbai liang, gebi A'er buceng tou)

There isn't a stash of silver 300 feet below this spot, your neighbor Ah-Er did not steal it

A nervous person is bound to make mistakes

A man once buried a pile of silver to hide it. Nervous that it would be stolen, he left a sign saying, 'No silver is buried here.' Unsurprisingly, the silver was stolen, and all that was left beside the pile of dug-up dirt was a sign saying that his neighbour did not steal it.

Persian

مگر هفت ماهه بدنیا آمدی؟

(magar haft máheí be donyá ámadí)

Did you really come into the world in seven months?

Said to somebody who is impatient, the type of person who is too impatient to spend nine months in the womb before being born

Polish

Zjeść z kimś beczkę soli

Eating a barrel of salt with someone

Getting to know someone really well [It's not easy eating a barrel of salt, just as it's not easy getting to know someone]

Portuguese

É cor de burro quando foge

It's the colour of a donkey on the run

Something that's difficult to describe, eg mousey brown hair colour

Viajou na maionese

To travel in the mayonnaise

To live in cloud-cuckoo land

Há mouros na costa
There are Moors on the coast
There is something threatening nearby

The Portuguese and Spanish of the Iberian Peninsula lived in fear of invasion by the Moors for many centuries.

Peixe não puxa carroça
(Brazilian Portuguese)
Fish don't pull wagons
The true meat-eater's motto

This is common in parts of Brazil (cattle country), where a 'real meal' has to include meat.

Quechua

Ima ayni mana kutichina

What *ayni* isn't caused to return?

You scratch my back, I'll scratch yours

> *This means 'What debt is not repaid? Anything you do for me, I will of course do for you – and vice versa'. Ayni can mean 'reciprocal labour', 'vengeance' or 'debt'.*

Qhapaqkay ichiykachay, wakchakay kumuykachay

To be rich is to stand tall, to be an orphan is to bend over

The rich man holds his head high, the poor man stoops

> *This is an observation, made in the Andes, about how wealth brings pride and poverty beats you down.*

Manchay kamachikuq, mana mikhuchikuq

Fear gives orders, but doesn't feed

Overworked and underpaid [A boss is good at giving orders, but not at feeding you]

Romanian

A vinde gogosi

To sell pastries

To tell lies [Both pastries and lies are full of hot air]

Russian

Уйти несолоно хлебавши

(oo-i-ti nye-so-la-na khlye-baf-shee)

To leave after an unsalted meal

To get nothing for your efforts

Открыть Америку

(at-kryt' a-mye-ree-koo)

To discover America

To state the obvious

Spanish

Va de Guatemala hacia Guatapeor

It's going from Guatemala to Guatapeor

It's going from bad to worse

In Spanish mala *means 'bad' and* peor *means 'worse', so this expression is a play on words, a bit like saying 'from Baden-Baden to Worsen-Worsen'.*

Cebollento

Oniony

Used to describe the overwrought love ballads sung by male Latin American singers

The songs are described as 'oniony' because of the false tears shed by the singers during their performances. Women may not use this expression but their husbands/boyfriends would.

Tragado como media de cartero

(Colombian Spanish)

Swallowed like the postman's sock

Hopelessly in love

Tragado *(swallowed)* is slang for 'in love' as well as 'sucked in'. A postman who walks around all day eventually has his socks sucked into his shoes.

Swedish

Han/Hon har rent mjöl i påsen

He/She has clean flour in his/her sack

He/She is honest and trustworthy

Att sätta myror i huvudet på någon

To put ants in someone's head

To confuse someone to the extent that it feels like ants running around his/her head

Att skära guld med täljkniv

To cut gold with a pocket knife

To make a lot of money with very little effort

Det är ingen ko på isen (så länge bakbenen står på land)

There's no cow on the ice (as long as its hind legs are on land)

There's no need to panic

Thai

เห็นช้างขี้ ขี้ตามช้าง

(hěn cháhng kêe kêe đahm cháhng)

Seeing an elephant shit or shitting like an elephant

Emulating the actions of others, especially those who are in a higher social or economic situation than you, ie bigger than you

ย้อมแมวขาย

(yórm maa-ou kǎi)

Dyeing the cat to sell it

Patching up inferior goods to pass them off as something better

ปิดทองหลังพระ

(bìt torng lǎng prá)

Pasting gold leaf onto the back of the Buddha image

Doing a good deed in secret, without making a show of it

Turkish

Balık baştan kokar

Fish smells from the head

Corruption starts at the top

Eşeğin kuyruğunu kalabalıkta kesme, kimi uzun der kimi kısa

Don't cut off the donkey's tail in public – some will say it's too long, some will say it's too short

You can't satisfy everyone

Ayağının altına karpuz karbuğu koymak

To put a watermelon skin under someone's foot

To cause someone's downfall; To cause someone to be ousted from office

There once was a woman-chasing muezzin, who every time he climbed the minaret to make the call to prayer, would ogle the women below. People began to get fed up with this and came up with a plan to teach him a lesson. They placed some watermelon skin on the stairs of the minaret. When the muezzin came down the stairs he slipped and tumbled all the way to the bottom. When he finally got out of hospital, he took up work as a vegetable seller, and never ascended a minaret staircase again.

ACKNOWLEDGMENTS

Publisher: **Roz Hopkins**

Commissioning Editors: **Laetitia Clapton & Karin Vidstrup Monk**

Project Manager: **Bridget Blair**

Editor: **Annelies Mertens**

Researcher: **Lou Callan**

Design & Layout: **Annika Roojun & Gerilyn Attebery**

Illustrations: **Theresa Hamilton**

Thanks also to: **Karina Coates, Karina Dea, Nick Forward, Mark Germanchis & Jane Pennells**

This book is largely the result of contributions by many Lonely Planet readers and friends. We'd like to thank the following people for contributing their favourite expressions:

99mpritt, Andra, anolazima, babygiraffe, Daniela Bertoglio, Kay Baker, Richard Barker, Charlie Beech, Annette & Noel Callan, Matthew Callan, Minu Chawla, chrissy, CecileM, Neil Clancy, Tony Cleaver, Francesca Coles, confucius, Astrid Cybulskis, Erika Cybulskis, Peter Cybulskis, Rita Cybulskis, dagi, dara, Barbara Delissen, Hilko Drude, ericavisser, esponga, eti,

Jamie Evans, Andy Gibbons, Carol Greig, fabio, felis, flatfoot, fly1ngkiwi, frogger, grecophile, GuilleBaires, Ben Handicott, Des Hannigan, hasof, higgins, igor, Indiana_Girl, javox, kalimero, kape, Karyn674, Kate James, katfive, Russell Keen, Helen & Mark Kenny, kiomera, Michaela Klink, koenie, koolhass, kurzschluss, littlefish, Bernadette Lonergan, marmotte, Donna McCormick, Annelies Mertens, meydl, Mideast3003, Marija Minic, Minna_P, mistaprez, Catriona Morrison, Rose Mulready, naniwako, neu-roticat, Olli_HKI, oropendola, Fabrice Rocher, Tom Parkinson, PiesDescalzos, Jan Pisek, Anuj Raina, Duane Ruth-Heffelbower, Ayla Sabine Sevim, Annie Schwartz, Andrew Smith, smith-sgj, John Soos, sprite, supersinga, T8M, thinduke, tlmy69, Zachary Treisman, Karin Vidstrup Monk, Sasha Wajnryb, wordplayer, xoai, zashibis, Monica Zavoianu, zelgadis, J. Zvirgzdgrauds

We'd also like to thank the following people and organisations for their expertise in verifying the expressions in this book:

Yoshi Abe, Mohamed Al-Samsam, Khosrow Azordegan, Gus Balbontin, Rose Barbosa, Tilman Berger, Roni Bieri, S. Breandán Ó hUallacháin, Ines Callalli, Erez and Jane Cohen, Francesca Coles, CreoleTrans, Yavgar Dehgheni, Mark Dinneen, Stephanie Di Trocchio, Elisabet Eir Cortes, Corne & Dan Foster, Irene Elmerot, Bruce Evans, Mary Fitzpatrick,

Quentin Frayne, David Frye, Peter Friedlander, Tilahun Gabriel, Denise Gardiner, Ben Handicott, Paul Hellander, Errol Hunt, Garry Hunt, Gordana Ivetac, Birgit Jordan, Piers Kelly, Robert Lagerberg, Joy Lagumay, Dick Littlebear, Liz Lopez, Marta López, Maltese Community Council of Victoria, Kruno Martinac, Jim & Peri Masters, Stephen Matthews, Christina Mayer, Melbourne Latvian Society, Elizabeth Minchin, Kammy Mok, Marcia Monje de Castro, Prima Nusawati, Sylvie Polge, Gerald Porter, Penelope Richardson,Michael Sawer, Gerdi Schumann, Andrew Siedlecki, Slovenian Australian Institue, Trinh Vu, Clara Yim of Chin Communications, Christina Zarifopol-Illias

If you pick up any other expressions on your travels, why not note them here?

You can send your favourites to us at *saywhat@lonelyplanet.com*
If we publish your expressions in a subsequent edition of the book, you will get a free copy.

Have fun!